Making the Most of Your Sabbatical Leave

*An Essential Guide
to Taking a Career Break
(or Sabbatical)
to Rejuvenate Your Life
While Using Time Wisely*

by Michael Newton

Table of Contents

Introduction

The word "sabbatical" comes from the Greek "sabbatikos," which means "of the Sabbath." The Greeks in turn got it from the Hebrew "shabbat," which means "to cease."

Did you know that the Bible literally commands people to take a Shabbat from work? Since God took a Shabbat after spending six days creating the world, the same was ordained for ordinary people. The Bible also made it clear that even slaves and beasts of burden deserved a Shabbat from their labors, but it didn't stop there.

God told Moses to "sow your fields for six years, for six years prune your vineyards and gather their crops. But in the seventh year the land is to have a year of Shabbat rest, a Shabbat to the Lord. Do not sow your fields or prune your vineyards. Do not reap what grows of itself or harvest the grapes of your untended vines. The land is to have a year of rest." (Leviticus 25: 3-5)

Whether or not you're Christian, you have to admit that's sound ecological and agricultural advice right there. The land is to get a break from human interference every seventh year. The Bible wasn't talking about crop rotation. It was talking about a complete Shabbat from any deliberate tilling and growing.

A sabbatical leave (let's just say "sabbatical" from now on, alright?) was originally granted to university professors after six years. It was meant to give them a chance to broaden their horizons beyond the classroom, grant them a much needed break, and prevent them from suffering burn out.

Since it worked with many teachers, some organizations and companies began to follow suit. To differentiate sabbaticals from extended vacations, and to avoid any religious connotations, however, most prefer to call them 'strategic job pauses' or 'long leaves.'

Whether you're a teacher or a company executive, you're probably excited by the prospect of a sabbatical. Considering how long and how hard you've worked, you certainly deserve it, so congratulations! This book will provide plenty of suggestions on how to maximize this wonderful opportunity.

Unfortunately, many who are considering a sabbatical only look at the time off involved, seemingly unaware that sabbaticals carry potential risks which can impact their career, their reputation, and their income. This book will therefore also cover the potential pitfalls that accompany taking a sabbatical, providing suggestions as for how to best deal with them so you can maximize your sabbatical as much as possible.

Chapter 1: Understanding the Economics

While sabbaticals are offered by many European and Canadian organizations, the sad fact is that few American ones do. According to the US Bureau of Labor Statistics, only about 20% offer some sort of extended paid leave not related to the accumulated leaves that all employees are legally entitled to.

Few small universities can afford to give their teachers year-long sabbaticals, however. While a number of the bigger and better off ones do provide an entire year, they're usually (but not always) given with half pay.

The most others get is a guarantee of a job when they return. If teachers want to take an entire year off, most have to do so at their own expense.

In these trying economic times, even the Ivy Leagues have begun to cut back. According to the American Association of University Professors, sabbaticals are often the first to go when the economy gets rough.

Teachers unions have tried to protect sabbaticals, but in light of the poor economy and after Governor Scott Walker passed Act 10 in Wisconsin (which severely weakened the power of public-employee unions), there's little they've actually been able to do. Others, especially in Republican-dominated states, have chosen to lie low in order to protect what they already have.

Still other campuses have begun reviewing their sabbaticals because they have been abused. Professors who go away sometimes "find themselves," join a commune (or another university) somewhere, and never return. Others return completely out of touch with their topics, and still others fail to provide an adequate replacement in their absence. This not only leaves the university in a lurch, it also makes students suffer.

Others believe that because they have tenure and because they've done their six years, they're automatically entitled to a sabbatical. These have failed to understand the terms of their employment contract. Worse, they don't understand the procedures and negotiations involved. As a result, they fail to meet them.

Research sabbaticals are another matter entirely. These are done for work related purposes, usually to another organization or university. Since the economic benefits, experience gained, and status brought, have direct and measurable effects, these tend to be granted more easily. A number of universities have begun referring to these as Professional Development Awards. They still involve work, however, and if you play your cards right, it'll come with decent pay.

So we have a poor economy, less well-off organizations, and better-off ones that have become less generous. As of 2015, what does all that mean for you?

Chapter 2: Keeping in Mind a Few Pre-Sabbatical Warnings

There are two major things you have to consider before heading off on your sabbatical, or before you think of availing of one:

Less income or no income

Be prepared to cut back and dig deeper into your savings. Of those who go on a year-long sabbatical with half pay or none, about a quarter end up cutting their sabbaticals short or taking a part time job elsewhere to pay the bills.

For those who are single, this isn't too much of a problem. They only have themselves to look out for, after all. But for those with a family to support (and assuming their partners don't earn enough), it's another ball game entirely.

Some believe that going on sabbatical to a less-developed country will stretch their dollars further. While this is technically true, they ignore the extra expenses involved in moving to and living in another country.

There's also the dreaded higher currency syndrome. It's called by many different things, but it refers to the madness people experience when they go to a developing nation and discover just how far $100 can go (very far in some places, but not all).

Professional and personal disruption

If you can afford to go on sabbatical with your friends and family, then you should have no problems. They might even enjoy it.

But since sabbaticals are about breaking away from routine, they do have a major impact on your career. If you do consulting work as a sideline, for example, a year can be a very long time. With corporate attrition rates at an all time high, the connections you made at various companies could have moved on. By the time you get back, you run the risk of having to rebuild your network and your reputation up again from scratch.

Nor can you afford to ignore office politics. In an ideal world, education, teaching, and work in general exist for their own lofty sakes. Unfortunately, such a world never was or likely will be. A promotion, position, or raise you may be thinking about could go to someone else in your absence. This could set your own prospects back by several years.

Universities, like all organizations, are run by people, after all. And everyone is a political being—whether or not they admit it or even realize it. That includes you. Fortunately, there are some things you can do to protect yourself or mitigate the impact.

Chapter 3: Taking Care of What You Leave Behind

Be informed

The problem with easy and free downloads is that we've learned to just click "Accept" without bothering to read the fine print. When it comes to employment contracts, however, that can be dangerous; especially if you're due for a sabbatical (or think you are).

Harvard University was the first to give out sabbaticals in 1880, but not all universities have followed suit, or have since stopped doing so. Kent State University used to have them, but stopped in 2009 because of money. Though they later reinstated it, they've been quite stingy about them. Iowa is currently under pressure to end sabbaticals for all state universities.

Do your research

If your facility can't (or won't) fund your sabbatical, don't despair. There are quite a number of organizations out there who provide help with such things. Among these are **Fulbright** (http://eca.state.gov/fulbright) and **Guggenheim** (http://www.gf.org/about/fellowship/) fellowships. If you're in the medical field, the **National Institutes of Health** (NIH) (http://www.nih.gov/) is a research agency that provides support through its **Academic Research Enhancement Award** (AREA) (http://grants.nih.gov/grants/funding/area.htm) program.

If these are willing to shell out money for you, then you're set. All you need from your school is a guarantee that your job will still be waiting for you when you get back. Obviously you'll have to plan and apply several years ahead.

Stay in touch

You have an obligation to return to your organization. As such, it's best to stay in touch, and if relevant, to provide them with updates about what's happening with you. Updates allow your organization to know that their investment in you is paying off. Even if it's unpaid or partially paid, your organization will at least know that you have every intention of going back to work.

Do the same for those you do consulting work for. Let them know when you're leaving and when to expect you back. Also keep in touch so they don't forget about you. This is especially important if you don't want to start again from scratch upon your return.

Some professors who get paid sabbaticals stay in touch with their students, as well as with whoever is substituting for them. This doesn't mean you have to stay in touch full time. A conference call or answering email every few weeks will do. If you choose this option, remember that you're on sabbatical so make sure everyone knows what that means. In case you forget, it means saying "nope, I'm not available except on…"

Keeping your employers, co-employees, and students in the loop has the added benefit of allowing you to transition more easily back to what you left behind. It also serves as a reminder that your sabbatical will come to an end so you'd better make the most of it.

Family matters

While some sabbaticals are spent at home or near it, most who avail of them prefer to travel. If you have a spouse who can't take time off, this can be a problem. It's even worse, however, when dealing with small children. If you're leaving them behind with friends and family, then good for you! What else are they for, after all?

But if you insist on bringing them along, you'll face two major problems: day care for toddlers and schooling for the older ones. Both require money, so that's another factor you have to consider. Here's another one: vaccination. That's another expense right there.

For older kids, there's also the issue of schedules. Are you taking them along before their final exams? If you're going to dump them in summer camp, will you be able to get back in time to pick them up again? If you want them to study abroad, be sure to find out about their scholastic schedules because not everyone follows our system.

Did you know that Berkeley, MIT, Harvard, and Stanford provide daycare services? Yes, even for those on a sabbatical. The downside is that they require you to get on their list a full 18 months ahead.

The better you know about these things and can arrange for them ahead of time, the more you can focus on your sabbatical.

The dangers of re-entry

This is not something often discussed, but a look at teacher's forums shows that it's quite common. Although many are very passionate and dedicated about what they do, a number find the thought of going back to work difficult, especially if they've managed an entire year off.

For some, sabbaticals change their lives because it allows them to explore other career paths and lifestyle options they'd never had the courage (or the means) to experience before. As such, they return to work only because of their contract or because they have no other choice because of financial reasons.

Still others realize they love what they do, but not where they've been doing it or how they've been doing it. Yet others end their sabbaticals brimming with new ideas, but are unsure if these will work in their old setting. And of course, there are those who just want their sabbaticals to go on for various reasons, often personal.

For those who've kept in regular touch, going back is not usually hard. If you do find the thought of going back difficult, simply accept that this is natural and that many go through it. Not just here in America, but elsewhere, even in countries where sabbaticals are far more common than here.

If you still find the idea of going back very challenging, then you might have to make some life-changing decisions.

Chapter 4: Standing Firm on Going on a Sabbatical

Well, thank goodness! You should.

Most who go on a sabbatical say it was worth the hassles, expense (or lack thereof), and effort involved. Even those who decided not to return to their organizations found the experience worthwhile.

The problem with routines (besides the boredom involved) is that it sometimes blinds us to what's out there. This can result in poor performance and a limited outlook. It can also narrow a person's horizons, not just from an emotional and intellectual perspective, but from a professional standpoint, as well.

Others also benefit from your sabbatical. What may be mundane to you could be inspirational to others and vice-versa. You could hold the missing key that others have been looking for. It's even possible that your sabbatical could result in the next breakthrough the world has been waiting for with bated breath.

There are stories galore of professors who return with groundbreaking ideas, of corporate executives coming back with a new vision for their companies, of managers brimming with enthusiasm and boosting their team's output.

Some savvy companies even mandate sabbaticals because it gives them an edge over their competitors, since time off ranks higher than salary as an attractive benefit to potential employees. Also, people generally like to buy from and support entities that treat their employees well—a good pitch you could use if you're asking for a sabbatical. Still others provide them as a means of retaining valued employees (be careful with this particular pitch, though).

While you can certainly liaise with others around the world through the internet, nothing beats real face-to-face meetings. It's why major companies like Google and Yahoo have begun cutting back on work-at-home options for their employees. Not only did working online decrease employee creativity, but it apparently had a negative impact on overall productive output, as well.

Research has also shown that taking a sabbatical could be good for your physical and mental health.

Faculty members from universities around the world claimed to have increased satisfaction levels, reduced stress, and a more positive outlook. They also tended to become even more loyal to their organizations, as a result.

There were also those who discovered alternative sources of income. Still others found better ways to channel their energies, while a good number found real-world applications for their knowledge set and skills.

So yes, you should go, but how should you maximize yours? Fortunately, there's quite a bit of information out there on this topic.

Chapter 5: Remaining Focused

You're meant to take a break and are allowed to have fun. You should recuperate, take care of your health or that of family and friends. And certainly there's nothing wrong with lounging about a gorgeous beach while sipping piña coladas.

But unless you plan to retire for good, you should stay focused. This means your sabbatical should in some way be related to what you do. If you're an engineering professor, for example, working at an engineering firm to get hands-on experience about the industry would be best.

The problem many companies have today is that our colleges keep churning out graduates who are in no way, shape or form prepared for the work force. Only the fast-food industry has no complaints, but they tend to pay non-survivable wages.

So when planning your sabbatical, think of what it is you really want to achieve. Travel is nice, resting is great, and so is sleeping till late afternoon. But also consider how much you're getting, how much you'll have to dig into your pockets, and plan accordingly.

It helps to start an automatic savings plan, preferably one with decent interest rates. If you're going to travel, make arrangements for your utilities to be paid and maximize your income by renting or subletting your place. Then consider how far your available income will go when choosing your destination.

Sabbatical Homes

(https://www.sabbaticalhomes.com/) is a great resource if you're planning to travel. They arrange home swaps for academics. This not only allows you to control your budget, it also lets you get some insider info about the place from those you'll be swapping with.

The downside is that their places are currently limited only to some cities in the US, Canada, Australia, as well as London and Paris. Still, if those are your destinations, it can't hurt to give them a try.

If you're staying put, one thing most professors and managers are unanimous about is this: stay away from your campus or office! It's so easy to fall back into old habits, the last thing you want to do on a sabbatical.

Whatever you teach or do, there's something out there related to your line of work. If you teach African-American history, for example, visit Ghana. **Cape Coast Castle** (http://theculturetrip.com/africa/ghana/articles/ghana-s-slave-castles-the-shocking-story-of-the-ghanaian-cape-coast/) specializes in tours explaining their involvement in the American slave trade.

It overlooks some spectacular beaches, too. And since Ghana has historically been closely linked with the western world, you can enjoy piña coladas at any of the five-star hotels that dot the coast. In case you were wondering, it costs about $11 a day to live in Ghana.

A professor who studies American Indian populations once took her sabbatical in Australia where she studied Aboriginal peoples. Though the cultures are vastly different, it gave her new perspectives on her subject matter, expanded her personal horizons, and provided her with new insights on the topic of indigenous peoples.

A drama professor used her sabbatical to open a theater group. She wanted to apply her knowledge and be involved in her community, not just limit herself to the academe.

If you're on a sabbatical to finish a book or a thesis, take the time to visit your subject matter, if possible, and meet those involved if you can. It's not absolutely necessary, of course.

Some take time off to be exposed to new ideas or experiences they can later use in their work, to engage in research opportunities not available at their institution, to study at other universities, or even to challenge themselves by trying out something completely different.

Whatever the case, those who approve of your sabbatical will be expecting something extra from you upon your return. Your inability to deliver that something extra could have a negative impact on future applications for sabbaticals.

In Canada and Europe, most require a post-sabbatical report from their teachers of what they'd been up to and what it is they'd accomplished. Companies which offer sabbaticals do the same.

Whatever you do, remember that sabbaticals are not vacations.

Chapter 6: Planning Ahead

Many sabbaticals have ended before they've even begun because of various reasons. The most common, however, has to do with relationships, especially those regarding spouses, kids, and scheduling.

While it would be great to do your sabbatical in Venice (Italy, not the beach in Florida), budget and scheduling conflicts can sometimes get in the way. Most sabbaticals are flexible, however, so you should be too.

If all you can get is something in the next city, then go for it. But if you're staying at home, then maximize it. Many confess that they spend the first day (or two) of their sabbatical just cleaning up their inboxes.

There are four main things you want to stick to as much as possible:

1) Stick to your budget, which has already been covered. Be sure to do your research on

exchange rates if you're traveling abroad, as well as on cost of living.

2) Determine your departure date and how long you'll be gone or unavailable. Stick to it, as well, because while sabbaticals are desirable, they're also among the easiest things to put off.

3) Tell others about it so they can provide suggestions, if any. It will also give them the opportunity to begin adapting to your absence or non-availability.

4) Shut off. If you're not leaving, that means staying away from your campus or office, even if you'll stay in touch.

Also write out a bucket list of things you want to accomplish:

1) Do you want to finish a project you've been putting off because you haven't had the time?

2) Do you want to pursue other career options or opportunities?

3) Do you want hands-on experience regarding your topic?

4) Do you want to study at another facility?

5) Do you want access to resources not available to your institution?

6) Do you want to do volunteer work? If so, then for what, whom, and why?

You can of course add to that list depending on your situation. Sometimes, the very uncertainty of what they want to achieve scares some off from taking a sabbatical. The more you know what you want out of it, the better you can stay focused on it.

Chapter 7: Learning to Be Flexible

Sometimes, the best things come about because of faith, the ability to trust that things will turn out alright. In order for this to happen, however, a degree of flexibility is required.

A corporate executive once confessed that she had spent her three month sabbatical learning how to rock climb. When asked what value that brought to her company, she said it taught her the value of taking on a challenge, how to strategize and plan, as well as manage risk. Overall, it also helped to improve her leadership style.

A Spanish teacher at a Canadian school travelled to Spain for an intensive language immersion course. Unfortunately, she ended up being unhappy with the institute. So in the evenings, she took up flamenco (a style of dance) and on the weekends, she took up cooking classes. She claims it opened her eyes up to nuances in the language that she had never known about, despite being born to a family of Mexican immigrants.

There was also an American professor of classical art who travelled to France expecting to work at a prominent museum there for the summer. Due to a serious miscommunication, however, he got there only to discover that the temporary position had been given to someone else. Even more unfortunate, his university was not paying for his sabbatical since they thought the museum was going to take care of that bit.

Rather than go home, he swallowed his pride and found work as a waiter (which pays an actual wage in France) to make ends meet. Thanks to that job, he met many locals and was exposed to the city's modern art scene, as well as to its less savory counterfeit art industry.

This allowed him to expand his understanding of the subject matter, be exposed to the practical side of the industry, improve his French, and better relate to his younger students. As to the staff and older students he left behind, they were shocked to discover he had a "cool" side.

These examples show that learning doesn't necessarily have to come from a structured plan. The ability to be open and to adapt to changing situations can go a very long way. Plans are there only to provide structure and some sort of guide.

Any well-heeled traveler will tell you that the key to success lies in three things:

1) The ability to travel light. The more you take with you, the less your ability to adapt becomes. Traveling light is not just about the amount of luggage you bring with you, however. It also refers to what you carry in your head.

It is both arrogant and unforgivable to go to a new setting and expect them to adapt or to conform to your idea of how things should be. It also closes you off to new ideas and to other ways of doing things, which is what you're supposed to learn when you go on a sabbatical.

2) The ability to balance structure with spontaneity. This was already covered, but it needs a separate portion because it's so important. Whether you're on a research sabbatical, an educational one, an "I just really need a break, or else" one, or even one for corporate purposes, you have a chance to see more of the world... even if it's just in another city or state.

It would be a shame to deny yourself new opportunities and experiences just because of some bucket list you've written out for yourself. Reserve that hotel, book that tour, and rent that car, certainly. You deserve comfort and some measure of stability, after all.

But once you've secured them, let your hair loose and have fun. You're on a sabbatical!

3) The ability to accept that you can't do it all. Chapter 5 was all about focusing on your goals, so how does that mesh with spontaneity? Even if you were given a chance to live in Paris for a year, you'll never see or experience it all. Not even those who've lived there their entire lives do.

The Spanish teacher balanced her Spanish language courses with local dance and cuisine, but she would surely have burned out if she also tried to take up scuba diving, hang gliding, art, volunteering, etc. You can't possibly see or do it all, so just accept that and focus on those things that interest you and that are within reach.

It would be a shame to return from your sabbatical needing a vacation because you're so exhausted.

Chapter 8: Staying Up-to-Date

This is especially important if you want to return to your job or be employable when your sabbatical ends. Our world is changing rapidly, so it's easy to become irrelevant. Some who return to their employers find that they've had to settle for a lower position with lower pay.

On midnight of May 5, 2015, oDesk changed its name to Upwork, for some reason, creating a lot of unhappy people. When Microsoft launched Windows 8.1 in late 2013, they killed the Start menu, changed the layout, and created even more unhappy people.

But that's the way it goes.

However you spend your sabbatical, don't just stay in touch with friends and colleagues. Make it a point to also keep up with the news, changing technologies, as well as the latest trends—especially those regarding your line of work.

According to a 2014 survey of hiring managers in the US, 61% said that up-to-date skill sets was their top consideration when choosing candidates. An awareness of industry-related info was the second. There's no point hiring someone to write for a tech blog if they're still using the old Windows 8 and therefore struggle with the new layout in 8.1, now is there?

With technology and events happening so fast in our increasingly connected world, you can't risk being a Rip Van Winkle. In case you forgot, he slept for 20 years and woke up to find his wife dead, his children grown, and America no longer a British kingdom but an independent republic.

And be sure to network while you're away. Social media is no longer about keeping in touch with or rediscovering old friends and family. It's also a way of staying relevant and maintaining employment or financial prospects.

Even if you go on sabbatical to get away, collect those calling cards, give out your own, and sell yourself, even if you can't take on new work right away. It's called passive marketing. Just letting others know that you're alive and what you do can open new opportunities for you.

Some find the thought of marketing themselves repugnant, but that's because they're hypocrites. You're either buying something (if only because you accept a point of view), or you're selling something (if only because you're trying to convince others about something).

Just don't go overboard or you'll turn people off.

Conclusion

No one knows why the God of the Bible thought the seventh day and the seventh year were special. But even He took a break, so you should, too.

It's your break, so how you spend it and what you do while on it is up to you. Go help the people in Haiti, learn rafting in the Grand Canyon, or ride a Venetian gondola. You could also stay home and finish that project you've been putting off for many years.

Whatever you do, remember that it should be productive. No one but you can decide what is or isn't useful on a sabbatical, but others will expect some change or some difference when you return.

That's the other thing you should remember about sabbaticals—they come to an end. So use your time wisely.

Finally, I'd like to thank you for purchasing this book! If you enjoyed it or found it helpful, I'd greatly appreciate it if you'd take a moment to leave a review on Amazon. Thank you!

Printed in Great Britain
by Amazon

21099405R00031